www.finishinglinepress.com

Too Many Seeds

poems by

Gabrielle Myers

Finishing Line Press
Georgetown, Kentucky

Too Many Seeds

ACKNOWLEDGMENTS

Poets and Writers: California Writers Exchange, 2009, "Damn Bird," First
Runner-up
MadHat Lit, October 2013, "Sonnet # 69"
Nebo, Winter 2011, "On Ayako Iino's 'Pa Amb Tomàquet'"
San Francisco Public Press, Spring 2011, "Quality Control"
Evergreen Review, Spring 2009, "To Bukowski" (originally published with
this title)
Wallace Stevens Journal, Spring 2015, "I am a Figure of Speech"
Work Literary Magazine, February 2014, "Prom Night"
Connecticut River Review, Summer 2018, "For Girls Who Walk to the Bus
Stop Alone"
Catamaran, Fall 2018, "Early Fall's Failed Elegy"
Borderlands: Texas Poetry Review, Fall 2021, "The Dried Fruit Factory: Dried
Bits"
Edible East Bay, Fall 2021, "Lidded," "On Ayako Iino's Pa Amb Tomàquet," and
"The Dried Fruit Factory: Harvest"

I would like to thank the following poets and writers for their mentorship and
guidance on the poems in this manuscript and on *Hive-Mind*, which I view as
a complimentary book of prose to *Too Many Seeds*: Brenda Hillman, Graham
Foust, Matthew Zapruder, Marilyn Abildskov, Pam Houston, Joe Wenderoth, Alan
Williamson, Rusty Morrison, Sandra McPherson, Cornelius Eady, Sharon Olds,
Claudia Rankine, and Josh Clover.

Publisher: Leah Huete de Maines
Editor: Christen Kincaid
Cover Art: Jill McLennan's, *Alameda, Then + Now*, www.jillmclennan.me
Author Photo: Jessica Myers
Cover Design: Elizabeth Maines McCleavy

Order online: www.finishinglinepress.com
            also available on amazon.com

Author inquiries and mail orders:
Finishing Line Press
P. O. Box 1626
Georgetown, Kentucky 40324
U. S. A.

Table of Contents

I.

Damn Bird

Do you hear me, bird?
Go swimming from cypress to dogwood
Electric winged and set to spring.
I can't know what goes and spins
In that wing,
Can't think what pulses tell you to turn
Or what noises send you
Out of your tree-met self.
Go and let me be,
Your song egging on a part of me
That ascends to collapse like a pollen-hung bee.

October

      Rows of tomatoes, leaf-heavy in their cages,
     lean toward creeping thyme like limp sentinels.
    Watermelon vines pinch metal fences with twisted runners.
  A Steller's jay gorges himself
on wounded ants and sugar-bloated aphids.

Fall, prodded from her tangle
  with keg parties, coconut suntan lotion, and grilled Red Hots,
    pulls herself away from long zucchini and flowering bolts of basil.
   No longer held back by preschoolers
    jumping on trampolines,
      she lands her cold paralysis
        on the blackened whorl of vines.

Hopeless

No more mulch to move.
No pine, oak, and eucalyptus shred
to spread for rose bushes, fig trees,
and birds of paradise all scraggly in summer's wane.
Her last day we hauled dry twiggy piles from the road
with her pickup truck. Hours were autumn,
our late afternoon silence.
Dust coated our lungs,
our hands' creases.
There was giving up
in how she pitch-forked mulch.
Dust bowed around her.

After these early rains, thistle and grass
begin to push into air
that weighs upon their infant green.
We know they will force their sheaths outward,
crowd the path to barn and gate.

Turn

Instead of fists and nails fighting in the dimly lit cabin,
your shadow waving, wings backed to nubs—

>You ran with father to the falls.
>The crickets made their clicks
>from behind birch and butterfly weed.
>You breathed in the gloaming,
>watched with fear the fissures on his face
>form quick like in a time-elapsed film.
>His eye-webs stretched, sagged from stress
>—a wrinkled sun-bitten fig—
>and you became as old
>as you are now,
>my forgiver.

Gathering Fennel Pollen

Beside a narrow highway cutting through shifted marsh fields,
each draw against umbrella-like stems
blackens my fingers, resin lozenges
ball between my joints.

Last year I threw my body into bushes,
pushed through seeding weeds' tall stalks,
ignored fears of rattlesnakes coiled near roadside streams
and ticks that might attach and bloom, lost in my long hair.

This year: plants on the field's edge.

Afternoon sun, gilded,
glinting off the bay, makes me squint,
focus on flowers in float-fall.

> I am thinking how to harvest,
> remembering how she showed me
> to move among branches.

My fingers touch miniature petal,
coarse stem, web threads
cast like fishing lines into gusty bay air.

Could nothing
have changed
her mind about living?

Look

Look,
just because you carry ecstatic leaves
and clatter with the urge and strain of storm wind
doesn't mean that others tremble,
bare for you
in the hot wax of summer,
probing bars and squares and parks
for the golden tunnel
your hand makes when full of seeds.

The Bee on the River

Sunning on the inner tube,
I saw a bee half submerged in the sluggish river.
Its torso in two worlds, one wing
Turned, a watermill off the surface.

The bee and I floated in two oceans.

I thought of cupping it in my hand,
Of lifting its waterlogged wing to dry on the tube.
I thought of her hands gripping fruit
Bruised from inside
By too many seeds.

Leaving Maryland

The air was sick in life,
Bloated with rain, ticks, and green earth.
Butterfly weed set out blooms—

                In seconds swallowtails sucked.
The creek climbed clay banks,

                Clinging like kudzu to tulip poplar.
Out in the fields, stillness

                Persisted despite a thunder-wind

                    Thrusting over hay tips.
Damn dampness descended
           Determined to etch the day.
I shook to grow
When spotted a tiger lily:
Immense.

After Niedecker

when ladybugs
       fall

from plum leaves
       that crowd
          the path

the sun

warming them
              as they sing

their tiny
       flimsy shells

Bomb Dream

After 9-11, After Orlando's Pulse Shooting, After Mass Shooting #1, 2, 3, 4, etc.

For many minutes we watch each drop hit the window;
                                    We don't become aware.
Time slivers itself against our cobweb-covered glass,
            Cuts the distance
                        between the bomb ticking on the road
                                                and us.
            You say: "There's nothing we can do."
            Dimes spin and drop into a puddle near our gutter;
            We think so much we hear their silver sides tip and splash.

Figs

If hornets catch in fig tangles,
Mingle fuzzy wings
Against fruit stretch's broad belly drops
(Sun-wrinkled in honey-suckled summer),
What is she left with, her ballasted street?
Pollen crumbs leave her stunned, stung.

Wouldn't one glisten and pull out a sting, if she's been stung?
Along the hay soiled path, Mission figs
Birth, knot in segments close to the street.
Each branch locks into the next,
Close as wings on a hornet's body.
(Dust pulls, eats honey in summer.)
I've seen her grasp for a loaded limb: her stretch

Lands bloated fruit in baskets. In that stretch,
A wish: Don't let her get in her own way, self-stung.
We harvest only in summer:
Leap for the fabled fig.
Don't we each have wings
When we want them? All the streets

We've left—can't we change thoughts like we turn streets?
The switch-backed mountains, clouded in buckeye, stretch
To Delta, and for all my potential muscle
And hover-flight, I'm stung.
Harvesting figs
In the grasshopper-tick of summer

Lifts, brings me to see what I didn't notice last summer…
The harbor sagged with moored sailboats, urine-misted streets
Sat in their driest hours, and the figs
I cut and mixed with arugula, pine nuts, balsamic stretched
On plate after plate. My index finger stung
By my paring knife, the wings

Of the fruit flew against steel and fell like all winged
Things to the bowl's birthing ground.
Was I stunted that summer,
Held in like a green swell?
I wanted to swim the crowded street.
Now, a bandage I make on her farm stretches
Around me as I reach: I am contained. Can figs

Be a sign, for her too? Like a stung street,
This harvest summer stretches:
Electric, winged, and opens its cut fruit.

Yuba River Regret

In you I swam naked,
as hamburgers blackened on a makeshift grill,
light beer got cool in the catastrophic water.
I was lean from working in the fields,
lapped your liquid between my lips like a brown trout.

Granite boulders held
their places in mud;
mica flecks lived their shine:

I tasted snow in you.

A million tiny turns,
you took the down-growing
course with ease,
pounded out your intent.

You knew—
it didn't take a seer
to know she would end herself.
There's no loving reflective
in your water
to incline the memory of her face,
just my quiet doubletalk,
and the need to shake.

Early Fall's Failed Elegy

Disproportion:
Her self taken by herself
to the remnant carpet's threads,
Remington rifle at her mud-winged boots,

> while the Christmas lima vines
> flourished, complicated the string trellises
> we spent an afternoon tying.
> The pods we pulled
> deflated, barren.

> Sparse rain was liquid for the watermelon.
> Charcoal orange in the sky,
> a peel burned for the tomatoes' negroni.

She wasn't the land, after.
Now, the Sacramento Valley
is the white siding of rushed housing,
crushed tomatoes on highway shoulders,
preschool soccer games in mowed-down plum orchards.
The sun, dry gold-straw,
turns into Sugar Pie pumpkin and Delicata squash.

> In memory, her sorrow
> shadowed by a tooth-full smile
> over eggplant bells, her lips and cheeks
> browning tough,
> loosening from her mind:
> a heavy fruit's skin
> separating from seed.

Fill

When we came home from the Bistro, little sparks tried to ignite in our hands, but were stopped by the doorknob's metal. Not like any other day because we tried not to fabricate, let our words fall where they gravitated to, inside us. I went into the study and sat at my desk. Sunlight filtered itself through the elm tree, through the pollen air, through the window streaked with spider webs. I did not write.

> What was it that we came toward,
> picking fennel fronds near aloe bloom towers?
> What it was that held her in her scene:
> shiny jade leaves soft in fog light.
> Thick knot to thick stem. How the plants
> grow grotesque in mild California.

Those years I did not write but made it a habit to think about what I could. No words stuck to me, nothing seemed to root. Only the spider plant, hung from the ceiling in that warehouse apartment, let its grounding roots spill into the air—so boney in sideways light. In early morning, the root ends would glisten with sap. I could not sleep.

> How the plants grow in California:
> Flower here, flower there,
> there a new leaf
> leaping towards fog, here a stem
> hardening in winter.

Mr. Rogers came on at 5:30 am. When the Jim Beam wore off, I woke up and stayed myself against the bed sheets, watched Mr. Rogers' green sweater and those hand puppets with threaded yarn hair. There was always singing.
Mr. Rogers knew how to comfort in the early morning.
Mr. Rogers knew he could bring even drunk girls in their 20's back to innocence. It had to do with the piano, with song. One hour, and I dozed until the summer's heat rose in my attic room, until I stuck to the flannel blanket I bought at CVS.

> My body cupped toward experience.
> A vessel?

Marlena liked to help me plant the tomatoes and zucchini. At first it was fun: I showed the girl how to dig, water the hole, dig some more, pinch the bottom leaves, lower the root ball into clay. Those gardening Sundays I started drinking early. In the sun, it felt right to have that cool bottle and its condensation in my hand.

As we pulled up crabgrass nets and threw them in the compost pile, she told me of her mom's brain tumor—it kept coming back, growing, hooking itself in. Marlena liked to pack the soil around transplants, make sure the leggy starts were fixed in the ground. At her birthday party, we ate pozole and her mom spooned ladle after ladle of the thin, red soup into blue bowls.

The next morning, I couldn't look at Marlena's little fingers—they were serpents, wriggling in the dirt, trying to life the weeds and tomatoes. The artichoke never flowered that summer, even the earthworms had tumors, curled on the soil surface, unable to burrow.

> Still there would come a time
> I didn't want that loneliness
> Staved it off with anything
> I could put inside.

Fog that would not go away lingered on the sticky bottlebrush tips and flaking window shutters. The morning Marlena, her two teenage brothers, and mother moved to East Oakland, I knew I would never see them again, never know how she turned out. She entered middle-school that fall, started wearing glasses that would cloud as she bent down to gather the oxalis seedlings threatening the new arugula crop.

In tone with her maturing breath and lengthening fingers, I knelt beside her and pulled thin spindly oxalis from their hold.

I write.
The spider loosens thread from his hind,
spills milky strands against the rusted window edge.
The cat that bites me when I try to pet it
falls asleep next to spiders, against the window.
He breathes the eye-stinging pollen air.

Whether I am filled or empty
does not matter.
I let the words fall.
Gravitate toward her.
Five years ago.
Little fingers like serpents in the Oakland soil.

Whether the syllables fill,
matters.

II.

On Ayako Iino's *Pa Amb Tomàquet*

There, nose, smell Ayako's meal.
There is afternoon, late August.
There is golden light that makes violet eggplants expand,
                    sends sugar into gypsy peppers.
There fog helps Black Plum tomatoes
                    dig for water,
                    coaxes them into pressurized drops of flavor.
There is salt sea, sardines swimming,
                    opalescent crisped skin,
                    briny flesh held in hand
                    —how it gives into her finger.
There, kelp, plankton, and sunlight through water.
There, her abandoned farm by the Sea of Japan,
pickled squid, Ume plums packed in salt,
a snapshot of her ex-husband and his young new wife at the door of a barn.
                    There, the year's first plum blossom
                    —a rain drop slipped from petal.
Haven't you dreamt you were in a plum orchard,
                    bare branches set to burst white?
Haven't you wondered about blossoming rows,
                    bees humming
                    when leaves fall and curl in the dry season?
There, nose, smell the basil she pinched from the garden plot in Oakland.
Smell her and her new husband working in the afternoon sun last March,
                    sweat-logged t-shirts,
                    compost from the kitchen,
                    orange peels resisting decay.
There, the fennel bulb she taught you to slice thin
                    so its fingers bend like a Buddha's Hand.
There, nose, a fermenting tomato left to rot beside a desiccated vine,
                    seeds meant to tumble in the soil, root next year.

Here Ayako peers into a vat black with hot oil.
She turns snapping squash blossoms with a slotted spoon.

Here, mouth, peppers caramelized in olive oil.
Here, mouth, tomatoes slow dried in a small oven.
Here, mouth, sardines still moist, barely set, pulled from thin bones.

Lidded

Detail how you caw and configure a single self.
Tell us how you put yourself
In there. Claim speech and hook the lip,
Maintain your place by saying
What sound you are.

Along the highway wild fennel, ground-tender,
Stiffens in passing car wind.
Motion beats it against the guardrail.
It gets tougher and bends less.
Summer stalks rail hard,
Their fronds lift up
Like a frustrated mother's forked palm.

In the fields we picked fragrant tomatoes:
Black Cherokee, Green Zebra, Sungold
—our hands itchy black resin.
Fava and pea vine greenness
Merged into tenacious eggplant veins,
Lengthened into pock marked tomatillos
(little fruit bells sheathed from sun)
Began to grow, overtake.

Rake yourself in like wind
Culls dead leaves from open fields.

The Dried Fruit Factory: Harvest

Coming to work in the pre-dawn,
I saw a company truck turned over
in a pelt of summer wheat,
its raisins lost to knee-high blades.

I Am a Figure of Speech

"I am myself a part of what is real, and it is my own speech and the strength of it, this only, that I hear or ever shall." "Figure of the Youth as Virile Poet,"
Wallace Stevens

Everywhere a part of what is real strengthens in its own speech.
Everywhere that speech shows its realness:
That verbena leaf detached from its stem speaks,
But like a rushed driver ignoring a walker in the crosswalk,
The leaf doesn't respond or change its path by what it sees.
A ground squirrel nibbles closer;
A jay flies before the verdant leaves
—there is no visual threat.

I should hear and speak the part of myself that is real,
This not only, but only this will strengthen me.
Only this will make speech spread over me.

My speech strengthens in a leaf
Detached from what is real.

Ungrafted

The basil sheaves, each meet by swaths ditched to grow,
And hoisted, peg us pitched to the plowman's blow.
We fetch an afternoon's gold, gild glinting toward
The bay-shore, hold and hang it by the hefty hinges
That make us raucous and round. How would we become
Without prediction? The muffler, a tail-pipe's pitcher,
Strikes our driveway's gravel rise—warm mutter sticks!
Extended gently, a new-laid mint's green arm rises.

Our fingers find invasive sunflowers, fondle all light
The ridge top can give. Each petal mourns a minion, but we
Harvest the tips, mass a bed in our hands. The summer forges
And hitches—its hammer rings canyons to a grasshopper's clap.
How to master things and not the self careening beneath bow-bends?
We, honeyed flies, appraise our clamor.

Their Fights After 45 Years of Marriage

Along the highway, golden rods get taken
                              down by snow melt.
Deep in that mountain-top wood
                              ponds thaw. Bottom-feeding fish
feel movement in their fins.

Haydn blasts from the speakers,
                              peaking trumpets near valley-rusted meadows,
                              descending deep near coal and shale mounds.

Dad and Mom sleep
                 in ascending winter light,
                              their grey hair sticks to head rests,
                              their glasses reflect the Poconos'
                              still alder towers.

Past the Water Gap, ice-shriveled terrain rises and rises,
stiff from its run from the sluggish Delaware.

Dig and Draw the Dawn

Vermillion triggers surround us: goal posts and flags ranked according to size,
Dear trinkets now lost to a creek's storm-heavy bend.
Rows align: soil ridges structure our thoughts of seeding.
Night severs the tail end of day: cricket chorus, chicken slumber.
Billions of bulbs send out subterranean feelers that buckle against quartz.
Here, plumes and pride have reign—we, queens of the chestnut bulge.
Things seem to have a place among wind-walks and our lovely behavior.
Hiding, a ladybug sets her mind on a chard's wilted heart.
Gliding, a turkey vulture bows and bends beyond a flower-crowded cliff.
Swing that hoe; dig in to unearth weed-wound nematodes.
Swallowtail wings, never steady, swerve toward warped cardboard.
Striding and plowing, a tractor has no ideas, only turns and turns.
Riding a machine takes patience. The slipped sky's air cages,
Kingdoms fallow and folded for our thighs to achieve.

Revival

Mallow takes vacant lots between here and San Pablo. Chicken wing bones catch flight when cast to rosemary bushes. I, awakening like a finger noticing seventy-nine textures on an orange rind,
am a windshield's shattered glass, a line of meth taken too hard in the nose, ten pills swallowed with a glass of whiskey.

> With the corpses I take up,
> lift to caress
> an oak leaf's torn side.

I dig for snails to steam and feel a heroin needle's point.
I am the kitchen where Adelino butchers sockets from stiff lamb legs,
the office where temps send template after template
to a CEO who's missed his Tahitian flight.
The growth goes on forever.
Beneath studio lofts, I finger bus change and listen to a bar mate's Cuervo-tinged whistle.
A word cleaves, troops, and clings to the bench's chipped paint.

The Dried Fruit Factory: Quality Control

In the factory
    men in reflective boots scrub scrub
    stains from the aster-blue floor,
    lean and twist their bodies to clean
    underneath lines once linked by uniforms and hair nets.
I watch: water   bleach clean   raisin-tint   iridescent spray

Plum-sized rats sneak through holes in the pipe-busy ceiling,
    feed on lost fruits,
           poisonous vapors pull their oiled bellies from factory bins.

Undocumented workers sweat,
touch pesticide-gassed fruits
through food safe gloves,
inhale I don't know how many
parts per million of methyl bromide.
             Pesticides hold in raisin skin,
skin still dusted,
       milky with natural yeast.

             Fifteen flatbeds full of families
             from Veracruz and Mazatlan,
             assigned to the plant
             by an employment agency.

      Pyramids of dried fruit, divided
      in boxes by the ounce or pound.
      Strawberries from China.
      Papaya from Thailand.
      Mangoes from Vietnam.
      Cut, combined,
      sold as mixed fruit "packed" in California.

Marshall Beach Trail, April

Seeded grasses onshore, tiny ticks, pop in the wind,
                    Cast by a blast toward the ice-plant's carpet.
            Cabbage moths scurry to hang themselves on each poppy before sunset.
            Orange petals flicker to awaken us.

Point to point we slouch to buffer ourselves from relentless wind.
Refreshed and blunted, climbing our way from edge to edge,
We mouth flecks of mint,
            Reach for Miner's lettuce seasoned with sea foam.
On the bay, one kayak and one motorboat
Stop to cull fat oysters from columned growth.

You say: "Let's go back, drive to the café."
You say nothing else. I say okay.
We stay for another minute.
            Wild oat grasses tick as they hit themselves.
            Coastal brush purrs, sweeping tough leaves back against themselves.
            Bells clang as cows gather on a hoof-razed, emerald hillside.

Sonnet #69

After John Berryman and Marianne Moore

Ceaselessly sullen, switch grass sacks fall:
Strike! We run for a strong love's body-beaten cover.
I lusk, you tramp, and the hummingbird draws
Sweetness from a limp trumpet flower. Ferocious,
You with that handle-rake, you comb my hair
Tangled by suppressed gestures, stamped
By a forearm with no damp cover.
"Who are you?" you stammer,
Callous and crotchety like a blimp that won't rise.

The woodpecker is our wood-warden,
And she culls us blistering to a pine's tenacious shade.
Pools of chips lay at our feet: vanilla burn.
Our smells melt in a comparable air.
Ant nests sink under our clinks,
And these worn fingers prod acorns to snug holes.

New Year's Day

We drive on a levee across the Delta.

I look down into dead marsh spears—none raise themselves from muck, only tangles of other weeds that never died back completely twist themselves up past spear crowns, attempt to make fog surface.

Things forgotten start to pop and bloom—corn thrown in an oiled skillet. In and beneath so much water   coldness   wind: the forgotten
assemble and thrust toward us, attempt to make an "us."

The Dried Fruit Factory: Dried Bits

Foam from a large hose:
serpentine coils near Fredrico's booted feet.
Chlorine air makes our lungs burn until tickled numb.
The fruit factory's thick steam: preservation.
Eduardo's fork lift's scratched ochre:
propane tank   plastic smolder   sugar crystals ignite.

Six steel conveyor belts hinge together under ten rows of cloudy fluorescents.
The packing line manager asks Juan, the box stacker, "necesita gasolina,
chingon?" Plastic wrap around each pallet mirrors our motion. Fruit refraction
delivered onto methyl bromide sprayed cargo trucks.

Beside the fruit cutting machine,
sulfured amber apricot bits
pressed by morning line-workers
still glisten through sanitizing solution.

The glycerin room's communal heat: sugar water steams into fruit. My heart
decorates each face with a desert of dangerous border stories. Body adjustments,
in which the conveyor belt rises from saguaro and organ pipe, clicking water
and steel sparks into red-dusted air. Beyond the ceiling fan, blue sky is kissed
with exhaust. No one there to tally.

Miguel comes with a paint scraper to lift
bloomed raisin bits from linoleum.
At the 17th hour of his 18-hour work day,
his nicked notched
knuckles, as culled
and cavernous as a walnut shell
in a San Joaquin orchard, push against
the floor, loosen the ground
and flattened fruits from their hold.

Astound light. Gather flies. Catch sun worn ears. Pin through earring holes
covered by hairnets.

Swerve

After Apollinaire

Fitful shaft, hold a now still fly
Once shaken in dusty fields
At the line where pasture turns from highway
Glistening sprouts abase your lips to grain
When you cast your words
I am lusterless up close
Come down like a dim candle
A miasma across your lips
Sudden like fruit's push
Hold still fly
Fitful shaft shaken in dusty fields
At the line where pasture turns from drought
Glisten sprouts abase my lips

Neither words nor grains

But an entire day's intensity
Held to a point with your candle
Recreate the tongue
Shore these panicked feet under a landscape
Still fly hold fitful shaft
At the line where swaths turn from buildings
Glisten sprouts abase my lips
Move through their churches
A miasma clouding your lyric step
Emerge as you stretch fragmented grains

The Dried Fruit Factory: Madrigal to the Factory

Greasy gravel puddles gather water drops.
            Theresa umbrellas her empty lunch bag,
                        waits for her ride, leans against our seething building.

Caramel fruit of sun,
            stay line-tight and dry,
                  lidded in wide containers.

Touch an oiled raisin's heat
            —preservation and commodity.
                  Touch the leveler's tacky brow,
                        shadow of the vine and weight of a grape.

Shadow of a vine and weight of the grape,
            factory fluorescents illumine our microwaved meal.
                Fans, belts, and pumps
                    incubate us.

The Dish Pit

Buttered rubber mats, slippery-stacked plates,
Larry's squamous hands move loose piles:
Chicken parts, parsnip puree, half-eaten orange rinds.
Goldfish in a reflecting pool leap
On pampas grass—their scales dry.

Grain

After Apollinaire

The river is grain to millers' hands
The swaths and ports distended
Swallows make grasses figurative
Every river is a wheat tip now
Separating quickly, dust from constellations
Phosphorescent wheat clogs tractor gears
And I am running I am hungry for allegory
In fright of the dry season's last thrust
Who rained switch-tails into my hair
Who ate the germ from my staple's shell

For Girls Who Walk Alone to the Bus Stop

For Sierra LaMar

To hear the highway's rush
as you turn away from the front door's shudder against its frame.

To smell cow dung, lavender moisturizing lotion,
and small weed tips fractured by frozen dew.

To think blackberry vine leaves
lead into the ditch's frost-raised soil,
$x=y - z/3,$
and you'll text Cassie back when you get on the bus.

To see the bus stop through two blocks
of sharply angled new development curbs,
through unblemished stucco and siding,
through salvia not yet bloomed and growing wide over sidewalks,
through pickup trucks spattered with the rainy season's host of bugs,
through sedans still waiting to start-up,
waiting for coffee steam to hit and fog windshields.

To hear the car behind,
his engine now idle,
feel him break,
smell his sweat as he forces you
—he's sticky and smells like Red Bull, doughnut glaze, clove cigarettes,
leather molded into skin through hours of driving.
To feel his hands:
their pull and push
singly shutting you.

Prom Night

and the kids from Palo Alto arrive in black Hummer limos.
Shed your dirty layer, wrinkled carrot!
Along the line, transparent orange peels and potato skins
get mashed onto mats by Larry's black boots.

Stiff walk. He's bent down to pull
hotel and sauté pans for forty years,
now his back refuses to bow for stainless steel.

       Salmon, lose that funky scale suit!
       Slide, slide along my blade. The white cutting board
       suits you, makes your pink flesh perk up in bleaching kitchen light.
       Now you cost 16.99 a #, and every cut I make carefully watched.
       Repeat after me, Fish: "I will contribute to the plate.
       I will be opalescent in my center.
       I will reveal the profundity of ocean river migration."

       Onions sweat in your juice, release into butter.
       Brown soft: caramelize sweet.

Nick scurries behind me to gather sauté pans
caked with Chanterelle beef sauce.
Ben slices each Flame grape into thirds
(Two hundred grapes in less than an hour).
Circular grape slices spread flat in hotel pans.
Soon, we'll make 140
grape, red oak leaf, goat cheese, and candied walnut salads.

For Bukowski

Blue bird walking in my heart
stop pecking at these tired ventricles
look at all the worms
writhing past my feet.

All Shouts Ring Whole on Festive Hands

Turn toward what can't be made out:
Isolate streets, creek water smooth before
Dividing stones: you, sprout singer.

A beginning: now mallow scouts:
Uncertain, you craft late night screen chores.
Turn toward what can't be made out.

A kettle blows until no steam comes from its spout:
Swallows brag to fight with winter: in flight-speech they soar.
Dividing stones, you, sprout singer.

Finally: winter rain rushes down muck for spring trout:
Face the chorus: yucca spears wash ashore:
Turn toward what can't be made out.

Why cry into a human shape: all shouts
Ring whole on festive hands: still, you ask what tore:
Dividing stones, you, sprout singer.

With all these paths to everyone, why question route:
A frame's fact hangs its door:
Turn toward what can't be made out—
Dividing stones, you, sprout singer.

The Dried Fruit Factory: Raisins: The Processing Line

Tapered surface line before descent:

        collapse, purple fruit; rush down belts,
            spill into plastic troughs.
    Flickering lights glisten,
    blanch vine color,
    shine on your wrinkled sides.
Build in the high turns,
    drop like leaf-tinted
        white water on the long-falling factory floor.
Gather:
    dampness holds you together,
            bloated.
    Months in stained crates:
    older batches cling, cling
    and loosen, cling and loosen.
    Weigh on each other until mold
    connects your dot like bodies.
Swell in clumps before steel turns:
    hover, jump
        over belts and machines,
until Sheila plunges her gloved hands into your swarm,
        pushes you down.

The March

In this throng of signs and hands and warm flesh,
Small beige stones grind under our feet.
An oriel takes seed from an empty bench.
Human sweat, body inches from body.
Two bodies up, a woman's hands fight
with wood's weight to keep her sign visible.
In the reflecting pool, our white shirts, our signs,
our white and black and mixed bodies.
Human sweat, each mixture of perfume, shampoo, moisturizer,
each plate of bacon, oatmeal, scrambled eggs,
each cup of orange juice and coffee,
sifts through our pores.
If I squint, I can see the reflecting pool's water
evaporate, pulled into the tulip poplar's tented leaves.

Memory

Tall grasses and ferns stilled
By humidity's weight. Clouds lower
Over birches' wispy branches. Creeks
Swollen from rain, push water
Down to Wyoming's saturated valley.
In his reclining chair,
Grandpa's right-hand trembles over firm leather.
Grandma's spoon knocks plastic,
Mixes orange juice concentrate with water.
Air conditioner's ignition and click,
Dry air's breath agitates fear lodged in my ankles.
In five years, all this will be gone.
I cull speech from my parched lips.

The Stroke

(Variation on a theme by Wallace Stevens, for Grandma)

At dusk, in the car, potholes and thistle skeletons
      Transform in the gloom, like pine trees
       Transform on a cow gutted hill.

    The Pocono's birch bones accelerate west.
    I remember her mottled skin, how her eyes
    Enlarged in proportion
    As she dwindled from chopped Jello and canned pears.

Thistle-eyed, insistent,
She could not speak,
But the birches cast their stripped stems
Toward abandoned coal mine shafts,
Transformed in the crepuscular light.
The spikes in her eyes leveled the room,
As she fidgeted with her wheelchair
And knocked her knee, smiling,
"I'll do it myself" and almost beat against the pane
To the birch's nicked trunks;
      It was action against diminishment.
She transformed in the bleached room,
      Transformed as the snow
        Transformed the road,
Transformed as her hand gripped her dinner tray,
      Transformed her body's pen,
Boisterous as the birches
    Flooded with her hands' plea.
Or was it the mine shafts' plea?

Out the dashboard, I watch how thistles
      pull themselves against low mists
       like she transformed in the room.
I watch how Sacramento's lights gather from the east,
      Build like the red bloom in her eyes,
And I remember the spikes,
      stripped stems lashing empty shafts.

Lunchtime View, March, Northern California

Out the second-floor office window, we see a truck spray fungicide on an almond orchard. Powder's wide cast pushes out of the spreader, lifts high into the air and comes down upon white blossoms. Blossoms are a week old, some overtaken by firm green leaves. Valley spring days, air stains with verdurous life; sun filters through emerging bugs and moist energy pulls from thin grass and weed. The Sutter Buttes, emerald, rise into sudden rock and height. Cars speed north over concrete, blossoms tangle in their windshield wipers. White powder walls spike above the trees' white crowns. Our poor bee, dizzy and spectral-like from powder and pollen, knocks the large glass widow; his fast jerk toward his orchard's reflection sends him to the circular asphalt driveway. The old farm truck shifts down each orchard row, its tires push mustard flowers back to their fleshy leaves.

April in Oakland

Plankton swims in the trout's gills
We storm ourselves in every loss
Flies leap from leaf-wet stacks
Damns open: swoosh she goes
Flies winnow warmth under our window's light
We storm ourselves in every loss

We storm ourselves in every loss
Streetlights flash: turn turn metal
Donut Deal hires on Saturday and our coffee's cold
Neon circuits cut us at stoplights
Swallows fly the Caldecott Tunnel

Streetlights flash: turn turn metal
And strawberries cast their pale green drops
Raider Girls promote the new Scion—nothing knee-high
Donut flour links with butter
We rise at dawn as well, eat donuts' plump sides

Strawberries cast their pale green drops
I'm filled with battalions that cut
A part of me when a loved one dies
Under the oil and smelt thick surface
A bloated steelhead glides, fat with glaze and flour
I'm filled with battalions that cut

You Can't Stop Trying to Fly

A something broken too far to mend by conventional ways
Can resurrect under unpredictable light.
Look at the pigeon with a missing leg;
Watch how it leaps, hovers, flies
To run under a crimson-smoked sky.
Boney nub finds ancestry
In ascendance, taps
In charcoal blessed air to find its burned leg.
What hover for a limb's home?
What leap for fleeting hind?
How can you stop
Fly a whole you,
Never really fractured enough;
The fight in
Not extinguished?

A Hummingbird and Our Orange Tree

The orange tree has been flowering for six days.
Day and night, breath moves
                        its bright perfume into our kitchen and living room.
As we scrub hardened sweet potatoes, caked chicken fat,
                        we hear constant bee-traffic,
                                wings hit stiff white flowers,
                                        petals fall to dry dirt.

Our cat's carpeted play-structure's platform sets straight to tree;
        she sits and stares at bees pull pollen,
                frenetically race to each blossom.

Even with the screen set firm in its frame,
        at night a small screw-sized moth lands on the window, and our cat hums,
                places her left paw at its white body,
careful to lick the moth's underside with her rough tongue.

Last night as I put away our cold spring risotto,
                        a small hummingbird danced beneath blossoms.
In the moon's dark half-crested light and our weak kitchen fluorescent,
                her wings and body flapped,
                        unhummingbird-like,
                                until she set her beak to extract
                                        the last pollen from a yielding flower.

Seal

The car ticking miles—fennel flowers
By thistle pins by mini golf centers.
The visual cues keep us locked
In light's sealed vision.
What we know, we tuck into a day.
Each night stitches slip out,
Make our skin-fabric billow.
Experience isn't ours.
We're not here, when there's
There under the thin peel of someone beside us,
Under the shadow-line of one
Who has seen what we could say.

On 70 Outside of Nicolaus, CA

Night lights and flute music—
darkness between towns,
between small housing developments on the highway.
At 80 mph, I pull the car's air in:
breath cast back for breath.
What does it mean when I stop
imagining what it would feel like
to be the person who lives in that house or the next,
to be that other person?

Notes:

The last two lines in "Turn" are adapted from lines in Margaret Atwood's poem "Waiting."

Each line's last word in G.M. Hopkins's "The Windhover" is my first in "Dig and Draw the Dapple-Dawn," starting from the end of his poem and working toward the beginning.

Gabrielle is a Professor of English, writer, and chef living in the Sacramento Valley of California. Gabrielle's memoir, *Hive-Mind*, details her time of love, awakening, and tragic loss on an organic farm. Her poetry manuscripts have been top finalists for the *Catamaran West Coast Poetry Prize* (2018 & 2020) and the *42 Mile Press Poetry Award (2014)*. Her poetry has been published in *The Adirondack Review, San Francisco Public Press, Fourteen Hills, Evergreen Review, pacificREVIEW, Connecticut River Review, Catamaran, Edible East Bay,* and *Borderlands: Texas Poetry Review*. She has led writing workshops for the Pacific Writing Conference at the University of the Pacific, Word Spring in Chico, and San Joaquin Valley Writers, and participated in a panel at the Great Valley Bookfest. Access links to her memoir, published poems, essays, articles, interviews, YouTube cooking channel, and seasonal recipe blog through her website: www.gabriellemyers.com

CPSIA information can be obtained
at www.ICGtesting.com
Printed in the USA
FSHW012336071221
86695FS

9 781646 627080